The Romanization of Roman Britain

F. Haverfield

Alpha Editions

This edition published in 2023

ISBN : 9789357942089

Design and Setting By
Alpha Editions
www.alphaedis.com
Email - info@alphaedis.com

Contents

PREFACE

The following paper was originally read to the British Academy in 1905, and published in the second Volume of its Proceedings (pp. 185-217) and in a separate form (London, Frowde). The latter has been sometime out of print, and, as there was apparently some demand for a reprint, the Delegates of the Press have consented to issue a revised and enlarged edition. I have added considerably to both text and illustrations and corrected where it seemed necessary, and I have endeavoured so to word the matter that the text, though not the footnotes, can be read by any one who is interested in the subject, without any special knowledge of Latin.

F. HAVERFIELD.

OXFORD, April 22, 1912

CHAPTER I

THE ROMANIZATION OF THE EMPIRE

Historians seldom praise the Roman Empire. They regard it as a period of death and despotism, from which political freedom and creative genius and the energies of the speculative intellect were all alike excluded. There is, unquestionably, much truth in this judgement. The world of the Empire was indeed, as Mommsen has called it, an old world. Behind it lay the dreams and experiments, the self-convicted follies and disillusioned wisdom of many centuries. Before it lay no untravelled region such as revealed itself to our forefathers at the Renaissance or to our fathers fifty years ago. No new continent then rose up beyond the western seas. No forgotten literature suddenly flashed out its long-lost splendours. No vast discoveries of science transformed the universe and the interpretation of it. The inventive freshness and intellectual confidence that are born of such things were denied to the Empire. Its temperament was neither artistic, nor literary, nor scientific. It was merely practical.

Yet if practical, it was not therefore uncreative. In its own sphere of everyday life, it was an epoch of growth in many directions. Even the arts moved forward. Sculpture was enriched by a new and noble style of portraiture. Architecture won new possibilities by the engineering genius which reared the aqueduct of Segovia and the Basilica of Maxentius.[1] But these are only practical expansions of arts that are in themselves unpractical. The greatest work of the imperial age must be sought in its provincial administration. The significance of this we have come to understand, as not even Gibbon understood it, through the researches of Mommsen. By his vast labours our horizon has broadened beyond the backstairs of the Palace and the benches of the Senate House in Rome to the wide lands north and east and south of the Mediterranean, and we have begun to realize the true achievements of the Empire. The old theory of an age of despotism and decay has been overthrown, and the believer in human nature can now feel confident that, whatever their limitations, the men of the Empire wrought for the betterment and the happiness of the world.

[Footnote 1: Wickhoff, *Wiener Genesis*, p. 10; Riegl, *Stilfragen*, p. 272.]

Their efforts took two forms, the organization of the frontier defences which repulsed the barbarian, and the development of the provinces within those defences. The first of these achievements was but for a time. In the end the Roman legionary went down before the Gothic horseman. But before he fell he had done his work. In the lands that he had sheltered, Roman civilization had taken strong root. The fact has an importance which we to-day might easily miss. It is not likely that any modern nation will soon again stand in the place that Rome then held. Our culture to-day seems firmly planted in three continents and our task is rather to diffuse it further and to develop its good qualities than to defend it. But the Roman Empire was the civilized world; the safety of Rome was the safety of all civilization. Outside was the wild chaos of barbarism. Rome kept it back from end to end of Europe and across a thousand miles of western Asia. Through all the storms of barbarian onset, through the carnage of uncounted wars, through plagues which struck whole multitudes down to a disastrous death, through civil discord and sedition and domestic treachery, the work went on. It was not always marked by special insight or intelligence. The men who carried it out were not for the most part first-rate statesmen or first-rate generals. Their successes were those of character, not of genius. But their phlegmatic courage saved the civilized life of Europe till that life had grown strong and tenacious, and till even its assailants had recognized its worth.

It was this growth of internal civilization which formed the second and most lasting of the achievements of the Empire. Its long and peaceable government—the longest and most orderly that has yet been granted to any large portion of the world—gave time for the expansion of Roman speech and manners, for the extension of the political franchise, the establishment of city life, the assimilation of the provincial populations in an orderly and coherent civilization. As the importance of the city of Rome declined, as the world became Romeless, a large part of the world grew to be Roman. It has been said that Greece taught men to be human and Rome made mankind civilized. That was the work of the Empire; the form it took was Romanization.

This Romanization has its limits and its characteristics. First, in respect of place. Not only in the further east, where (as in Egypt) mankind was non-European, but even in the nearer east, where an ancient Greek civilization reigned, the effect of Romanization was inevitably small. Closely as Greek civilization resembled Roman, easy as the transition might seem from the one to the other, Rome met here that most serious of all obstacles to union, a race whose thoughts and affections and traditions had crystallized into definite coherent form. That has in all ages checked Imperial assimilation; it was the decisive hindrance to the Romanization of the Greek east. A few Italian oases were created by the establishment of *coloniae* here and there in Asia Minor and in Syria. But all of them perished like exotic plants.[1] The Romanization of these lands was political. Their inhabitants ultimately learnt to call and to consider themselves Romans. But they did not adopt the Roman language or the Roman civilization.

[Footnote 1: Mitteis, *Reichsrecht und Volksrecht*, p. 147; Kubitschek, *Festheft Bormann* (Wiener Studien, xx. 2), pp. 340 foll.; L. Hahn, *Rom und Romanismus im griechisch-röm. Osten* (Leipzig, 1906).]

The west offers a different spectacle. Here Rome found races that were not yet civilized, yet were racially capable of accepting her culture. Here, accordingly, her conquests differed from the two forms of conquest with which modern men are most familiar. We know well enough the rule of civilized white men over uncivilized Africans, who seem sundered for ever from their conquerors by a broad physical distinction. We know, too, the rule of civilized white men over civilized white men—of Russian (for example) over Pole, where the individualities of two kindred and similarly civilized races clash in undying conflict. The Roman conquest of western Europe resembled neither of these. Celt, Iberian, German, Illyrian, were marked off from Italian by no broad distinction of race and colour, such as that which marked off Egyptian from Italian, or that which now divides Englishman from African or Frenchman from Algerian Arab. They were marked off, further, by no ancient culture, such as that which had existed for centuries round the Aegean. It was possible, it was easy, to Romanize these western peoples.

Even their geographical position helped, though somewhat indirectly, to further the process. Tacitus two or three times observes that the western provinces of the Empire looked out on no other land to the westward and bordered on no free nations. That is one half of a larger fact which influenced the whole history of the Empire. Round the west lay the sea and the Sahara. In the east were wide lands and powerful states and military dangers and political problems and commercial opportunities. The Empire arose in the west and in Italy, a land that, geographically speaking, looks westward. But it was drawn surely, if slowly, to the east. Throughout the first three centuries of our era, we can trace an eastward drift—of troops, of officials, of government machinery—till finally the capital itself is no longer Rome but Byzantium. All the while, in the undisturbed security of the west, Romanization proceeded steadily.

The advance of this Romanization followed manifold lines. The Roman government gave more or less direct encouragement, particularly in two ways. It increased the Roman or Romanized population of the provinces during the earlier Empire by establishing time-expired soldiers—men who spoke Latin and who were citizens of Rome[1]—in provincial municipalities (*coloniae*). It allured provincials themselves to adopt Roman civilization by granting the franchise and other privileges to those who conformed. Neither step need be ascribed to any idealism on the part of the rulers. *Coloniae* served as instruments of repression as well as of culture, at least in the first century of the Empire. When Cicero[2] describes a *colonia*, founded under the Republic in southern Gaul, as 'a watch-tower of the Roman people and an outpost planted to confront the Gaulish tribes', he states an aspect of such a town which obtained during the earlier Empire no less than in the Republican age. Civilized men, again, are always more easily ruled than savages.[3] But the result was in any case the same. The provincials became Romanized.

[Footnote 1: English writers sometimes adduce the provincial origins of the soldiers as proofs that they were unromanized. The conclusion is unjustifiable. The legionaries were throughout recruited from places which were adequately Romanized. The auxiliaries, though recruited from less civilized districts, and though to some extent tribally organized in the early Empire, were denationalized after A.D. 70, and non-Roman elements do not begin to recur in the army till later. Tiberius *militem Graece testimonium interrogatum nisi Latine respondere vetuit* (Suet. *Tib.* 71).]

[Footnote 2: Cic. *pro Font.* 13. Compare Tacitus, *Ann.* xii. 27 and 32, *Agr.* 14 and 32.]

[Footnote 3: Tacitus emphasizes this point. *Agr.* 21 *ut homines dispersi ac rudes, eoque in bella faciles, quieti et otio per voluptates adsuescerent, hortari privatim adiuvare publice ut templa fora domos exstruerent…. Idque apud imperitos humanitas vocabatur, cum pars servitutis esset.*]

No less important results followed from unofficial causes. The legionary fortresses collected settlers—traders, women, veterans—under the shelter of their ramparts, and their *canabae* or 'bazaars', to use an Anglo-Indian term, formed centres of Roman speech and life, and often developed into cities. Italians, especially of the upper-middle class, merchants and others,[1] emigrated freely and formed tiny Roman settlements, often in districts where no troops were stationed. Chances opened at Rome for able provincials who became Romanized. Above all, the definite and coherent civilization of Italy took hold of uncivilized but intelligent men, while the tolerance of Rome, which coerced no one into conformity, made its culture the more attractive because it seemed the less inevitable.

[Footnote 1: The best parallel to the Italian emigration to the provinces during the late Republic and early Empire is perhaps to be found in the mediaeval German emigrations to Galicia and parts of Hungary (the Siebenbürgen Saxons are an exception), which Professor R.F. Kaindl has so well and minutely described. The present day mass emigration of the lower classes is something quite distinct.]

The process is hard to follow in detail, since datable evidence is scanty. In general, however, the instances of really native fashions or speech which are recorded from this or that province belong to the early Empire. To that age we can assign not only the Celtic, Iberian, and Punic inscriptions which we find occasionally in Gaul, Spain, and Africa, but also the use of the native titles like Vergobret or Suffete, and the retention of native personal names and of that class of Latin *nomina*, like Lovessius, which are formed out of native names. In the middle Empire such things are rarer. Exceptions naturally meet us here and there. Punic was in almost official use in towns like Gigthis in the Syrtis region in the second century, and Punic-speaking clergy, it appears, were needed in some of the villages of fourth-century Africa. Celtic is stated to have been in use at the same epoch among the Treveri of eastern Gaul—presumably in the great woodlands of the Ardennes, the Eifel and the Hunsrück.[1] Basque was obviously in use throughout the Roman period in the valleys of the Pyrenees. So in Asia Minor, where Greek was the dominant tongue, six or seven other dialects, Galatian, Phrygian, Lycaonian, and others, lived on till a very late date, especially (as it seems) on the uncivilized pastoral areas of the Imperial domain-lands.[2] Some of these are survivals, noted at the time as exceptional, and counting in the scales of history for no more than the survival of Greek in a few modern villages of southern Italy or the Wendish oasis seventy miles from Berlin. Others are more serious facts. But they do not alter the main position. In most regions of the west the Latin tongue obviously prevailed. It was, indeed, powerful enough to lead the Christian Church to insist on its use, and not, as in Syria and Egypt, to encourage native dialects.[3]

[Footnote 1: Jerome, *Comment. in epist. ad Galatas*, ii. 3. His assertion has, however, met with much scepticism in modern times, and it must be admitted that he was not a very accurate writer.]

[Footnote 2: K. Holl, *Hermes*, xliii. 240-54; William M. Ramsay, *Oesterr. Jahreshefte*, viii. (1905), 79-120, quoting, amongst other things, a neo-phrygian text of A.D. 259; W.M. Calder, *Hellenic Journal*, xxxi. 161.]

[Footnote 3: Mommsen (*Röm. Gesch.* v. 92) ascribes the final extinction of Celtic in northern Gaul to the influence of the Church. But the Church was not in itself averse to native dialects, and its insistence on Latin in the west may well be due rather to the previous diffusion of the language.]

In material culture the Romanization advanced no less quickly. One uniform fashion spread from the Mediterranean throughout central and western Europe, driving out native art and substituting a conventionalized copy of Graeco-Roman or Italian art, which is characterized alike by its technical finish and neatness, and by its lack of originality and its dependence on imitation. The result was inevitable. The whole external side of life was lived amidst Italian, or (as we may perhaps call it) Roman-provincial, furniture and environment. Take by way of example the development of the so-called 'Samian' ware. The original manufacture of this (so far as we are here concerned) was in Italy at Arezzo. Early in the first century Gaulish potters began to copy and compete with it; before long the products of the Arretine kilns had vanished even from the Italian market. Western Europe henceforward was supplied with its 'best china' from provincial and mainly from Gaulish sources. The character of the ware supplied is significant. It was provincial, but it was in no sense unclassical. It drew many of its details from other sources than Arezzo, but it drew them all from Greece or Rome. Nothing either in the manner or in the matter of its decoration recalled native Gaul. Throughout, it is imitative and conventional, and, as often happens in a conventional art, items are freely jumbled together which do not fit into any coherent story or sequence. At its best, it is handsome enough: though its possibilities are limited by its brutal monochrome, it is no discredit to the civilization to which it belongs. But it reveals unmistakably the Roman character of that civilization.

The uniformity of this civilization was crossed by local variations, but these do not contradict its Roman character. If the provincial felt sometimes the claims of his province and raised a cry that sounds like 'Africa for the Africans' he acted on a geographical, not on any native or national idea. He was demanding individual life for a Roman section of the Empire. He was anticipating, perhaps, the birth of new nations out of the Romanized populations. He was not attempting to recall the old pre-Roman system. Similarly, if his art or architecture embodies native fashions or displays a local style, if special types of houses or of tombstones or sculpture occur in special districts, that does not mar the result. These are not efforts to regain an earlier native life. They are not the enemies of Roman culture, but its children— sometimes, indeed, its adopted children—and they signify the birth of new Roman fashions.

It remains true, of course, that, till a language or a custom is wholly dead and gone, it can always revive under special conditions. The rustic poor of a country seldom affect the trend of its history. But they have a curious persistent force. Superstitions, sentiments, even language and the consciousness of nationality, linger dormant among them, till an upheaval comes, till buried seeds are thrown out on the surface and forgotten plants blossom once more. The world has seen many examples of such resurrection—not least in modern Europe. The Roman Empire offers us singularly few instances, but it would be untrue to say that there were none.

But while it is true generally that Romanization spread rapidly in the west, we must admit great differences between different districts even of the same provincial areas. Some grew Romanized soon and thoroughly, others slowly and imperfectly. For instance, Gallia Comata, that is, Gaul north and west of the Cevennes, contrasted sharply in this respect with Narbonensis, the province of the Mediterranean coast and the Rhone Valley. This latter, even in the first century A.D., had become *Italia verius quam provincia*. The other lagged behind. Neither the Latin speech nor the Latin forms of municipal government became quickly common. Yet even in northern Gaul

Romanization strode forward. The Gaulish monarchy of A.D. 258-73 shows us the position north of the Cevennes just after the middle of the third century. In it Roman and native elements were mixed. Its emperors were called not only Latinius Postumus, but also Piavonius and Esuvius Tetricus. Its coins were inscribed not only 'Romae Aeternae', but also 'Herculi Deusoniensi' and 'Herculi Magusano'. It not only claimed independence of Rome or perhaps equality with it, but it aspired to be the Empire. It had its own senate, copied from that of Rome; *tribunicia potestas* was conferred on its ruler and the title *princeps iuventutis* on its heir apparent. At that date it was still possible for a Gaulish ruler to bear a Gaulish name and to appeal to some sort of native memories. But the appeal was made without any sense that it was incompatible with a general acceptance of Roman fashions, language, and constitution. Postumus, if he had had the chance, would have made himself Emperor of Rome. Though the native element in Gaul had not died out of mind, at any rate its opposition to the Roman had become forgotten. It had become little more than a picturesque and interesting contrast to the all-absorbing Roman element. A hundred and thirty years later it had almost wholly vanished.

Such is the historical situation to which we must adjust our views of any single province in the western Empire. Two main conclusions may here be emphasized. First, Romanization in general extinguished the distinction between Roman and provincial, alike in politics, in material culture, and in language. Secondly, it did not everywhere and at once destroy all traces of tribal or national sentiments or fashions. These remained, at least for a while and in a few districts, not so much in active opposition as in latent persistence, capable of resurrection under the proper conditions. In such cases the provincial had become a Roman. But he could still undergo an atavistic reversion to the ancient ways of his forefathers.

CHAPTER II

PRELIMINARY REMARKS ON ROMAN BRITAIN

One western province seems to form an exception to the general rule. In Britain, as it is described by the majority of English writers, we have a province in which Roman and native were as distinct as modern Englishman and Indian, and 'the departure of the Romans' in the fifth century left the Britons almost as Celtic as their coming had found them. The adoption of this view may be set down, I think, to various reasons which have, in themselves, little to do with the subject. The older archaeologists, familiar with the early wars narrated by Caesar and Tacitus, pictured the whole history of the island as consisting of such struggles. Later writers have been influenced by the analogies of English rule in India. Still more recently, the revival of Welsh national sentiment has inspired a hope, which has become a belief, that the Roman conquest was an episode, after which an unaltered Celticism resumed its interrupted supremacy. These considerations have, plainly enough, very little value as history, and the view which is based on them seems to me in large part mistaken. As I have pointed out, it is not the view which is suggested by a consideration of the general character of the western provinces. Nor do I think that it is the view which agrees best with the special evidence which we possess in respect of Britain. In the following paragraphs I propose to examine this evidence. I shall adopt an archaeological rather than a legal or a philological standpoint. The legal and philological arguments have often been put forward. But the legal arguments are entirely *a priori*, and they have led different scholars to very different conclusions. The philological arguments are no less beset with difficulties. Both the facts and their significance are obscure, and the inquiry into them has hitherto yielded little beyond confident and yet wholly contradictory assertions and theories which are not susceptible of proof. The archaeological evidence, on the other hand, is definite and consistent, and perhaps deserves fuller notice than it has yet received. It illuminates, not only the material civilization, but also the language and to some extent even the institutions of Roman Britain, and supplies, though imperfectly, the facts which our legal and philological arguments do not yield.

I need not here insert a sketch of Roman Britain. But I may call attention to three of its features which are not seldom overlooked. In the first place, it is necessary to distinguish the two halves of the province, the one the northern and western uplands occupied only by troops, and the other the eastern and southern lowlands which contained nothing but purely civilian life.[1] The two are marked off, not in law but in practical fact, almost as fully as if one had been *domi* and the other *militiae*. We shall not seek for traces of Romanization in the military area. There neither towns existed nor villas.

Northwards, no town or country-house has been found beyond the neighbourhood of Aldborough (Isurium), some fifteen miles north-west of York. Westwards, on the Welsh frontier, the most advanced town was at Wroxeter (Viroconium), near Shrewsbury, and the furthest country-house an isolated dwelling at Llantwit, in Glamorgan.[2] In the south-west the last house was near Lyme Regis, the last town at Exeter.[3] These are the limits of the Romanized area. Outside of them, the population cannot have acquired much Roman character, nor can it have been numerous enough to form more than a subsidiary factor in our problem. But within these limits were towns and villages and country-houses and farms, a large population, and a developed and orderly life.

[Footnote 1: For further details see the Victoria County Histories of *Northamptonshire*, i. 159, and *Derbyshire*, i. 191. To save frequent references, I may say here that much of the evidence for the following paragraphs is to be found in my articles on Romano-British remains printed in the volumes of this History. I am indebted to its publishers for leave to reproduce several illustrations from its pages. For others I refer my readers to the History itself.]

[Footnote 2: See my *Military Aspects of Roman Wales*, notes 60 and 82. There was some sort of town life at Carmarthen.]

[Footnote 3: The Roman remains discovered west of Exeter are few and mostly later than A.D. 250. No town or country-house or farm or stretch of roadway has ever been found here. The list of discoveries includes only one early settlement on Plymouth harbour, another near Bodmin, of small size, and a third, equally small and of uncertain date, on Padstow harbour; some scanty vestiges of tin-mining, principally late; two milestones (if milestones they be) of the early fourth century, the one at Tintagel church and the other at St. Hilary; and some scattered hoards and isolated bits. Portions of the country were plainly inhabited, but the inhabitants did not learn Roman ways, like those who lived east of the Exe. Even tin-mining was not pursued very actively till a comparatively late period, though the Bodmin settlement may be connected with tin-works close by.]

[Illustration: FIG. 1. THE CIVIL AND MILITARY DISTRICTS OF BRITAIN.]

Secondly, the distribution of civilian life, even in the lowlands, was singularly uneven. It is not merely that some districts were the special homes of wealthier residents. We have also to conceive of some parts as densely peopled and of some as hardly inhabited. Portions of Kent, Sussex, and Somerset are set thick with country-houses and similar vestiges of Romano-British life. But other portions of the same counties, southern Kent, northern Sussex, western Somerset, show very few traces of any settled life at all. The midland plain, and in particular Warwickshire,[1] seems to have been the largest of these 'thin spots'. Here, among great woodlands and on damp and chilly clay, there dwelt not merely few civilized Roman-Britons, but few occupants of any sort.

[Footnote 1: *Victoria Hist. of Warwickshire*, i. 228.]

And lastly, Romano-British life was on a small scale. It was, I think, normal in quality and indeed not very dissimilar from that of many parts of Gaul. But it was in any case defective in quantity. We find towns in Britain, as elsewhere, and farms or country-houses. But the towns are small and somewhat few, and the country-houses indicate comfort more often than wealth. The costlier objects of ordinary use, fine mosaics, precious glass, gold and silver ornaments, occur comparatively seldom.[1] We have before us a civilization which, like a man whose constitution is sound rather than strong, might perish quickly from a violent shock.

[Footnote 1: See my remarks in Traill's *Social England* (illustrated edition, 1901), i. 141-61.]

CHAPTER III

ROMANIZATION IN LANGUAGE

We may now proceed to survey the actual remains. They may seem scanty, but they deserve examination.

First, in respect of language. Even before the Claudian conquest of A.D. 43, British princes had begun to inscribe their coins with Latin words. These legends are not merely blind and unintelligent copies, like the imitations of Roman legends on the early English *sceattas*. The word most often used, REX, is strange to the Roman coinage, and must have been employed with a real sense of its meaning. After A.D. 43, Latin advanced rapidly. No Celtic inscription occurs, I believe, on any monument of the Roman period in Britain, neither cut on stone nor scratched on tile or potsherd, and this fact is the more noteworthy because, as I shall point out below, Celtic inscriptions are not at all unknown in Gaul. On the other hand, Roman inscriptions occur freely in Britain. They are less common than in many other provinces, and they abound most in the military region. But they appear also in towns and country-houses, and some of the instances are significant.

The town site that we can best examine for our present purpose is Calleva or Silchester, ten miles south of Reading, which has been completely excavated with care and thoroughness. Here a few fairly complete inscriptions on stone have been discovered, and many fragments of others, which prove that the public language of the town was Latin.[1] The speech of ordinary conversation is equally well attested by smaller inscribed objects, and the evidence is remarkable, since it plainly refers to the lower class of Callevans. When a weary brick-maker scrawls SATIS with his finger on a tile, or some prouder spirit writes CLEMENTINVS FECIT TVBVL(*um*) (Clementinus made this box-tile), when a bit of Samian is marked FVR—presumably as a warning from the servants of one house to those of the next—or a rude brick shows the word PVELLAM—probably part of an amatory sentence otherwise lost—or another brick gives a Roman date, the 'sixth day before the Calends of October', we may be sure that the lower classes of Calleva used Latin alike at their work and in their more frivolous moments (Figs. 2, 3, 4). When we find a tile scratched over with cursive lettering—possibly part of a writing lesson—which ends with a tag from the *Aeneid*, we recognize that not even Vergil was out of place here.[2] The Silchester examples are so numerous and remarkable that they admit of no other interpretation.[3]

[Footnote 1: For these and for the following *graffiti* see my account in the *Victoria History of Hampshire*, i. 275, 282-4. For the 'Clementinus' tile (discovered since) see *Archaeologia*, lviii. 30. Silchester lies in a stoneless country, so that stone inscriptions would naturally be few and would easily be used up for later building. Moreover, its cemeteries have not yet been explored, and only one tombstone has come accidentally to light.]

[Footnote 2: Sir E.M. Thompson, *Greek and Latin Palaeography* (1894), p. 211, first suggested this explanation; *Eph.* ix. 1293.]

[Footnote 3: To call them—as did a kindly Belgian critic of this paper in its first published form—'un nombre de faits trop peu considérable' is really to misstate the case.]

[Illustration: FIG. 2. ... *puellam.*]

[Illustration: FIG. 3. *Fecit tubul(um) Clementinus.*]

[Illustration: FIG. 4. *vi K(alendas) Oct(obres)....*]

[Illustration: FIGS. 2, 3, 4. GRAFFITI ON TILES FROM SILCHESTER. (P. 25.)]

[Illustration: FIG. 5. GRAFFITO ON A TILE FOUND AT SILCHESTER (P. 25). *Pertacus perfidus campester Lucilianus Campanus conticuere omnes.* (Probably a writing lesson.)]

I have heard this conclusion doubted on the ground that a bricklayer or domestic servant in a province of the Roman Empire would not have known how to read and write. This doubt really rests on a misconception of the Empire. It is, indeed, akin to the surprise which tourists often exhibit when confronted with Roman remains in an excavation or a museum—a surprise that 'the Romans' had boots, or beds, or waterpipes, or fireplaces, or roofs over their heads. There are, in truth, abundant evidences that the labouring man in Roman days knew how to read and write at need, and there is much truth in the remark that in the lands ruled by Rome education was better under the Empire than at any time since its fall till the nineteenth century.

It has, indeed, been suggested by doubters, that these *graffiti* were written by immigrant Italians, working as labourers or servants in Calleva. The suggestion does not seem probable. Italians certainly emigrated to the provinces in considerable numbers, just as Italians emigrate to-day. But we have seen above that the ancient emigrants were not labourers, as they are to-day. They were traders, or dealers in land, or money-lenders or other 'well-to-do' persons. The labourers and servants of Calleva must be sought among the native population, and the *graffiti* testify that this population wrote Latin. It is a further question whether, besides writing Latin, the Callevan servants and workmen may not also have spoken Celtic. Here direct evidence fails. In the nature of things, we cannot hope for proof of the negative proposition that Celtic was not spoken in Silchester. But all probabilities suggest that it was, at any rate, spoken very little. In the twenty years' excavation of the site, no Celtic inscription has emerged. Instead, we have proof that the lower classes wrote Latin for all sorts of purposes. Had they known Celtic well, it is hardly credible that they should not have sometimes written in that language, as the Gauls did across the Channel. A Gaulish potter of Roman date could scrawl his name and record, *Sacrillos avot*, 'Sacrillus potter', on the outside of a mould.[1] No such scrawl has ever been found in Britain. The Gauls, again, could invent a special letter Đ to denote a special Celtic sound and keep it in Roman times. No such letter was used in Roman Britain, though it occurs on earlier British coins. This total absence of written Celtic cannot be a mere accident.

[Footnote 1: One example is *Sacrillos avot form.*, suggesting a bilingual sentence such as we find in some Cornish documents of the period when Cornish was definitely giving way to English. Another example, *Valens avoti* (Déchelette, *Vases céramiques*, i. 302), suggests the same stage of development in a different way.]

No other Romano-British town has been excavated so extensively or so scientifically as Silchester. None, therefore, has yielded so much evidence. But we have no reason to consider Silchester exceptional in its character. Such scraps as we possess from other sites point to similar Romanization elsewhere. FVR, for instance, recurs on a potsherd from the Romano-British country town at Dorchester in Dorset. A set of tiles dug up in the ruins of a country-house at Plaxtol, in Kent, bear a Roman inscription impressed by a rude wooden stamp (Fig. 6).[1] In short, all the *graffiti* on potsherds or tiles that are known to me as found in towns or country-houses are equally Roman. Larger inscriptions, cut on stone, have also been found in country-houses. On the whole the general result is clear. Latin was employed freely in the towns of Britain, not only on serious occasions or by the upper classes, but by servants and work-people for the most accidental purposes. It was also used, at least by the upper classes, in the country. Plainly there did not exist in the towns that linguistic gulf between upper class and lower class which can be seen to-day in many cities of eastern Europe, where the employers speak one language and the employed another. On the other hand, it is possible that a different division existed, one which is perhaps in general rarer, but which can, or could, be paralleled in some Slavonic districts of Austria-Hungary. That is, the townsfolk of all ranks and the upper class in the country may have spoken Latin, while the peasantry may have used Celtic. No actual evidence has been discovered to prove this. We may, however, suggest that it is not, in itself, an impossible or even an improbable linguistic division of Roman Britain, even though the province did not contain any such racial differences as those of German, Pole, Ruthene and Rouman which lend so much interest to Austrian towns like Czernowitz.

[Footnote 1: *Proc. Soc. Antiq. London*, xxiii. 108; *Eph.* ix. 1290.]

[Illustration: FIG. 6. FRAGMENT OF INSCRIBED TILE FROM PLAXTOL AND RECONSTRUCTION OF THE INSCRIPTION FROM VARIOUS FRAGMENTS. (The letters were impressed by a wooden cylinder with incised lettering, which was rolled over the tile while still soft. In the reconstruction CAB in line 2 and IT in line 3 are included twice, to show the method of repetition.)]

It remains to cite the literary evidence, distinct if not abundant, as to the employment of Latin in Britain. Agricola, as is well known, encouraged the use of it, with the result (says Tacitus) that the Britons, who had hitherto hated and refused the foreign tongue, became eager to speak it fluently. About the same time Plutarch, in his tract on the cessation of oracles, mentions one Demetrius of Tarsus, grammarian, who had been teaching in Britain (A.D. 80), and mentions him as nothing at all out of the ordinary course.[1] Forty years later, Juvenal alludes casually to British lawyers taught by Gaulish schoolmasters. It is plain that by the second century Latin must have been spreading widely in the province. We need not feel puzzled about the way in which the Callevan workman of perhaps the third or fourth century learnt his Latin.

[Footnote 1: See Dessau, *Hermes*, xlvi. 156.]

At this point we might wish to introduce the arguments deducible from philology. We might ask whether the phonetics or the vocabulary of the later Celtic and English languages reveal any traces of the influence of Latin, as a spoken tongue, or give negative testimony to its absence. Unfortunately, the inquiry seems almost hopeless. The facts are obscure and open to dispute, and the conclusions to be drawn from them are quite uncertain. Dogmatic assertions proceeding from this or that philologist are common enough. Trustworthy results are correspondingly scarce. One instance may be cited in illustration. It has been argued that the name 'Kent' is derived from the Celtic 'Cantion', and not from the Latin 'Cantium', because, according to the rules of Vulgar Latin, 'Cantium' would have been pronounced 'Cantsium' in the fifth century, when the Saxons may be supposed to have learnt the name. That is, Celtic was spoken in Kent about 450. Yet it is doubtful whether Latin 'ti' had really come to be pronounced 'tsi' in Britain so early as A.D. 450. And it is plainly possible that the Saxons may have learnt the name long years before the reputed date of Hengist and Horsa. The Kentish coast was armed against them and the organization of the 'Saxon Shore' established about A.D. 300. Their knowledge of the place-name may be at least as old. No other difficulty seems to hinder the derivation of 'Kent' from the form 'Cantium', and the whole argument based on the name thus collapses. It is impossible here to go through the whole list of cases which have been supposed to be parallel in their origin to 'Kent', nor should I, with a scanty knowledge of the subject, be justified in such an attempt. I have selected this particular example because it has been emphasized by a recent writer.[1]

[Footnote 1: Vinogradoff, *Growth of the Manor*, p. 102. I am indebted to Mr. W.H. Stevenson for help in relation to these philological points.]

CHAPTER IV

ROMANIZATION IN MATERIAL CIVILIZATION

From language we pass to material civilization. Here is a far wider field of evidence, provided by buildings, private or public, their equipment and furniture, and the arts and small artistic or decorative objects. On the whole this evidence is clear and consistent. The material civilization of the province, the external fabric of its life, was Roman, in Britain as elsewhere in the west. Native elements succumbed almost wholesale to the conquering foreign influence. In regard to public buildings this is natural enough. Before the Claudian conquest the Britons can hardly have possessed large structures in stone, and the provision of them necessarily came in with the Romans. The *fora*, basilicas, and public baths, such as have been discovered at Silchester, Caerwent and elsewhere, follow Roman models and resemble similar buildings in other provinces. The temples show something more of a local pattern (Fig. 7), which occurs also in northern Gaul and on the Rhine, but this pattern seems merely a variation of a classical type.[1] The characteristics of the private houses are more complicated. Their ground-plans show us types which, like the temples just mentioned, recur in northern Gaul as well as Britain, but which differ even more than the temples from the similar buildings in Italy, or indeed in the Mediterranean provinces of the Empire. The houses of Italy and of the south generally were constructed to look inwards upon open *impluvia*, colonnaded courts and garden plots, and, as befitted a hot climate, they had few outer windows. Moreover, they could be easily built side by side so as to form, as at Pompeii, the continuous streets of a town. The houses of Britain and northern Gaul looked outwards on to the surrounding country. Their rooms were generally arranged in straight rows along a corridor or cloister. Sometimes they had only one row of rooms (Corridor House, Fig. 8); sometimes they enclosed two or three sides of a large open yard (Courtyard House, Fig. 9); a third type somewhat resembles a yard with rooms at each end of it. In any case they were singularly ill-suited to stand side by side in a town street. When we find them grouped together in a town, as at Silchester and Caerwent—the only two examples of Roman towns in Britain of which we have real knowledge—they are dotted about more like the cottages in an English village than anything that recalls a real town (Fig. 10).

[Footnote 1: British examples have been noted at Silchester and Caerwent, and in many scattered sites in rural districts. For Gaulish instances, see Léon de Vesly, *Les Fana de région Normande* (Rouen, 1909); for Germany, *Bonner Jahrbücher*, 1876, p. 57, Hettner, *Drei Tempelbezirke im Trevirerlande* (Trier, 1901), and *Trierer Jahresberichte*, iii. 49-66. The English writers who have published accounts of these structures have tended to ignore their special character.]

[Illustration: FIG. 7. GROUND-PLANS OF ROMANO-BRITISH TEMPLES. CAERWENT
AND SILCHESTER.]

[Illustration: FIG. 8. GROUND-PLAN OF A SMALL CORRIDOR HOUSE FROM
FRILFORD, BERKSHIRE.

(*From plan by Sir A.J. Evans.*)]

[Illustration: FIG. 9. COURTYARD HOUSE AT NORTHLEIGH, OXFORDSHIRE, EXCAVATED IN 1815-16. (Room 1, chief mosaic with hypocaust; rooms 8-18, mosaic floors; rooms 21-7 and 38-43, baths, &c. Recent excavations show that this plan represents the house in its third and latest stage. See p. 31.)]

[Illustration: FIG. 10. DETAILED PLAN OF PART OF SILCHESTER. Showing the arrangement of the private houses and the Forum and Christian Church. (*From the plan issued by the Society of Antiquaries.*) (See p. 31.)]

The origin of these northern house-types has been much disputed. English writers tend to regard them as embodying a Celtic form of house; German archaeologists try to derive them from the 'Peristyle houses' built round colonnaded courts in Roman Africa and in the east. It may be admitted that the influence of this class of house has not infrequently affected builders in Roman Britain. But the differences between the British 'Courtyard house' and that of the south are very considerable. In particular, the amount of ground covered by the courts differs entirely in the two kinds of houses, while for the British houses of the plainer 'corridor' type the Mediterranean lands offer no analogies. We cannot find in them either *atrium* or *impluvium*, *tablinum* or peristyle, such as we find in Italy, and we must suppose them to be Roman modifications of really Celtic originals. This, however, no more implies that their occupants were mere Celts than the use of a bungalow in India proves the inhabitant to be a native Indian.[1]

[Footnote 1: *Vict. Hist. Somerset*, i. 213-14. A few Romano-British houses at Silchester (*in insula* xiv. (1), see *Archaeologia*, lv. 221) and at Caerwent (house No. 3, see *Arch.* lvii, plate 40) do bear some resemblance to the Mediterranean type, as I have observed in *Archaeol. Anzeiger*, 1902, p. 105. But they stand alone. Similarly, parallels may be drawn between Pompeian wall-paintings of houses and certain 'villa' remains in western Germany, as at Nennig; see Rostowzew, *Archaeol. Jahrbuch*, 1904, p. 103. But these again seem to me the exception.]

The point is made clearer by the character of the internal fittings, for these are wholly borrowed from Italian sources. If we cannot find in the Romano-British house either *atrium* or *impluvium*, *tablinum* or peristyle, such as we find regularly in Italy, we have none the less the painted wall-plaster (Fig. 11) and mosaic floors, the hypocausts and bath-rooms of Italy. The wall-paintings and mosaics may be poorer in Britain, the hypocausts more numerous; the things themselves are those of the south. No mosaic, I believe, has ever come to light in the whole of Roman Britain which represents any local subject or contains any unclassical feature. The usual ornamentation consists either of mythological scenes, such as Orpheus charming the animals, or Apollo chasing Daphne, or Actaeon rent by his hounds, or of geometrical devices like the so-called Asiatic shields which are purely of classical origin.[1] Perhaps we may detect in Britain a special fondness for the cable or guilloche pattern, and we may conjecture that from Romano-British mosaics it passed in a modified form into Later Celtic art. But the ornament itself, whether in single border or in many-stranded panels of plaitwork, occurs not rarely in Italy as well as in thoroughly Romanized lands like southern Spain and southern Gaul and Africa, and also in Greece and Asia Minor. It is a classical, not a British pattern.

[Footnote 1: It has been suggested that these mosaics were principally laid by itinerant Italians. The idea is, of course, due to modern analogies. It does not seem quite impossible, since the work is in a sense that of an artist, and the pay might have been high enough to attract stray decorators of good standing from the Continent. However, no evidence exists to prove this or even to make it probable. The mosaics of Roman Britain, with hardly an exception, are such as might easily be made in a province which was capable of exporting skilled workmen to Gaul (p. 57). They have also the appearance of imitative work copied from patterns rather than of designs sketched by artists. It is most natural to suppose that, like the Gaulish Samian ware—which is imitative in just the same fashion—they are local products.]

[Illustration: FIG. 11. RESTORATION OF PAINTED PATTERN ON WALL-PLASTER AT SILCHESTER. Showing a purely conventional style based on classical models. (P. 34.) (*From Archaeologia.*)]

Nor is the Roman fashion of house-fittings confined to the mansions of the wealthy. Hypocausts and painted stucco, copied, though crudely, from Roman originals, have been discovered in poor houses and in mean villages.[1] They formed part, even there, of the ordinary environment of life. They were not, as an eminent writer[2] calls them, 'a delicate exotic varnish.' Indeed, I cannot recognize in our Romano-British remains the contrast alleged by this writer 'between an exotic culture of a higher order and a vernacular culture of a primitive kind'. There were in Britain splendid houses and poor ones. But a continuous gradation of all sorts of houses and all degrees of comfort connects them, and there is no discernible breach in the scale. Throughout, the dominant element is the Roman provincial fashion which is borrowed from Italy.

[Footnote 1: R.C. Hoare, *Ancient Wilts, Roman Aera*, p. 127: 'On some of the highest of our downs I have found stuccoed and painted walls, as well as hypocausts, introduced into the rude settlements of the Britons.' This is fully borne out by General Pitt-Rivers' discoveries near Rushmore, to be mentioned below. Similar rude hypocausts were opened some years ago in my presence at Eastbourne.]

[Footnote 2: Vinogradoff, *Growth of the Manor*, p. 39.]

We find Roman influence even in the most secluded villages of the upland region. At Din Lligwy, on the northeast coast of Anglesea, recent excavation (Fig. 12) has uncovered the ruins of a village enclosure about three-quarters of an acre in extent, containing round and square huts or rooms, with walls of roughly coursed masonry and roofs of tile. Scattered up and down in it lay hundreds of fragments of Samian and other Roman or Romano-British pottery and a far smaller quantity of ruder pieces, a few bits of Roman glass, some Roman coins of the period A.D. 250-350, various iron nails and hooks, querns, bones, and so forth.[1] The place lies on the extreme edge of the British province and on an island where no proper Roman occupation can be detected, while its ground-plan shows little sign of a Roman influence. Yet the smaller objects and perhaps also the squareness of one or two rooms show that even here, in the later days of the Empire, the products of Roman civilization and the external fabric of Roman provincial life were present and almost predominant.

[Footnote 1: E. Neil Baynes, *Arch. Cambrensis*, 1908, pp. 183-210.]

[Illustration: FIG. 12. NATIVE VILLAGE AT DIN LLIGWY, ANGLESEA.]

[Illustration: FIG. 13. LATE CELTIC METAL WORK, NOW IN THE BRITISH
MUSEUM (1/3).

(*Boss of shield, of perhaps first century B.C., found in the Thames at Wandsworth, a little before 1850.*)]

CHAPTER V

ROMANIZATION IN ART

Art shows a rather different picture. Here we reach definite survivals of Celtic traditions. There flourished in Britain before the Claudian conquest a vigorous native art, chiefly working in metal and enamel, and characterized by its love for spiral devices and its fantastic use of animal forms. This art—La Tène or Late Celtic or whatever it be styled—was common to all the Celtic lands of Europe just before the Christian era, but its vestiges are particularly clear in Britain. When the Romans spread their dominion over the island, it almost wholly vanished. For that we are not to blame any evil influence of this particular Empire. All native arts, however beautiful, tend to disappear before the more even technique and the neater finish of town manufactures. The process is merely part of the honour which a coherent civilization enjoys in the eyes of country folk. Disraeli somewhere describes a Syrian lady preferring the French polish of a western boot to the jewels of an eastern slipper. With a similar preference the British Celt abandoned his national art and adopted the Roman provincial fashion.

He did not abandon it entirely. Little local manufactures of pottery or fibulae testify to its sporadic survival. Such are the brooches with Celtic affinities made (as it seems) near Brough (Verterae) in Westmorland, and the New Forest urns with their curious leaf ornament (Fig. 14),[1] and above all the Castor ware from the banks of the Nen, five miles west of Peterborough. We may briefly examine this last instance.[2] At Castor and Chesterton, on the north and south sides of the river, were two Romano-British settlements of comfortable houses, furnished in genuine Roman style. Round them were extensive pottery works. The ware, or at least the most characteristic of the wares, made in these works is generally known as Castor or Durobrivian ware. Castor was not, indeed, its only place of manufacture. It was produced freely in northern Gaul, and possibly elsewhere in Britain.[3] But Castor is the best known and best attested manufacturing centre, and the easiest for us to examine. The ware directly embodies the Celtic tradition. It is based, indeed, on classical elements, foliated scrolls, hunting scenes, and occasionally mythological representations (Figs. 15, 16). But it recasts these elements with the vigour of a true art and in accordance with its special tendencies. Those fantastic animals with strange out-stretched legs and backturned heads and eager eyes; those tiny scrolls scattered by way of decoration above or below them; the rude beading which serves, not ineffectively, for ornament or for dividing line; the suggestion of returning spirals; the evident delight of the artist in plant and animal forms and his neglect of the human figure—all these are Celtic. When we turn to the rarer scenes in which man is specially prominent—a hunt, or a gladiatorial show, or Hesione fettered naked to a rock and Hercules saving her from the monster[4]—the vigour fails (Fig. 17). The artist could not or would not cope with the human form. His nude figures, Hesione and Hercules, and his clothed gladiators are not fantastic but grotesque. They retain traces of Celtic treatment, as in Hesione's hair. But the general treatment is Roman. The Late Celtic art is here sinking into the general conventionalism of the Roman provinces.

[Footnote 1: For the New Forest ware see the *Victoria Hist. of Hampshire*, i. 326, and *Archaeol. Journal*, xxx. 319. The Brough brooches have been pointed out by Sir A.J. Evans, whose work on Late Celtic Art is the foundation of all that has since been written on it, but have not been discussed in detail.]

[Footnote 2: *Victoria Hist. of Northamptonshire*, i. 206-13; Artis, *Durobrivae of Antoninus* (fol. 1828).]

[Footnote 3: For the Belgic 'Castor ware' see the Belgian *Bulletin des commissions royales d'art et d'archéologie* (passim); H. du Cleuziou, *Poterie gauloise* (Paris, 1872), Fig. 173, from Cologne; *Sammlung Niessen* (Köln, 1911), plates lxxxvii, lxxxviii; Brongniart, *Traité des arts céram.*, pl. xxix (Ghent and Rheinzabern). M. Salomon Reinach tells me that the ware is not infrequent in the departments of the valleys of the Seine, Marne, and Oise. The Colchester gladiator's urn mentioning the Thirtieth Legion (C.R. Smith, *Coll. Ant.*, iv. 82, C. vii. 1335, 3) may well be of Rhenish manufacture.]

[Footnote 4: This, or the corresponding scene of Perseus and Andromeda, is a favourite with artists in northern Gaul and Britain. It occurs on tombstones at Chester (*Grosvenor Museum Catalogue*, No. 138) and Trier (Hettner, *Die röm. Steindenkmäler zu Trier*, p. 206), and Arlon (Wiltheim, *Luciliburgensia*, plate 57), and the Igel monument. For other instances see Roscher's *Lexikon Mythol.*, under 'Hesione'.]

[Illustration: FIG. 14. FRAGMENTS OF NEW FOREST POTTERY WITH LEAF
PATTERNS. (*From Archaeologia*).]

[Illustration: Fig. 15. URNS FROM CASTOR, NOW IN PETERBOROUGH MUSEUM.
(P. 41)]

[Illustration: FIG. 16. HUNTING SCENES FROM CASTOR WARE (ARTIS,
DUROBRIVAE). (SEE PAGE 41.)]

[Illustration: FIG. 17. HERCULES RESCUING HESIONE. (*From a piece of Castor ware found in Northamptonshire. C.R. Smith, Coll. Ant.*, vol. iv, Pl. XXIV.)]

A second instance may be cited, this time from sculpture, of important British work which is Celtic, or at least un-Roman (Frontispiece). The Spa at Bath (Aquae Sulis) contained a stately temple to Sul or Sulis Minerva, goddess of the waters. The pediment of this temple, partly preserved by a lucky accident and unearthed in 1790, was carved with a trophy of arms—in the centre a round wreathed shield upheld by two Victories, and below and on either side a helmet, a standard (?), and a cuirass. It is a classical group, such as occurs on other Roman reliefs. But its treatment breaks clean away from the classical. The sculptor placed on the shield a Gorgon's head, as suits alike Minerva and a shield. But he gave to the Gorgon a beard and moustache, almost in the manner of a head of Fear, and he wrought its features with a fierce virile vigour that finds no kin in Greek or Roman art. I need not here discuss the reasons which may have led him to add the male attributes to a properly female type. For our present purpose the important fact is that he could do it. Here is proof that, once at least, the supremacy of the dominant conventional art of the Empire could be rudely broken down.[1]

[Footnote 1: For the details of the temple and pediment see *Vict. Hist. Somerset*, i. 229 foll., and references given there. I have discussed the artistic problem on pp. 235 and 236.]

A third example, also from sculpture, is supplied by the Corbridge Lion, found among the ruins of Corstopitum in Northumberland in 1907 (Fig. 18). It is a sculpture in the round showing nearly a life-sized lion standing above his prey. The scene is common in provincial Roman work, and not least in Gaul and Britain. Often it is connected with graves, sometimes (as perhaps here) it served for the ornament of a fountain. But if the scene is common, the execution of it is not. Artistically, indeed, the piece is open to criticism. The lion is not the ordinary beast of nature. His face, the pose of his feet, the curl of his tail round his hind leg, are all untrue to life. The man who carved him knew perhaps more of dogs than lions. But he fashioned a living animal. Fantastic and even grotesque as it is, his work possesses a wholly unclassical fierceness and vigour, and not a few observers have remarked when seeing it that it recalls not the Roman world but the Middle Ages.[1]

[Footnote 1: *Arch. Aeliana*, 1908, p. 205. I owe to Dr. Chalmers Mitchell a criticism on the truthfulness of the sculpture.]

[Illustration: FIG. 18. THE CORBRIDGE LION. (P. 43.)]

These exceptions to the ruling Roman-provincial culture are probably commoner in Britain than in the Celtic lands across the Channel. In northern Gaul we meet no such vigorous semi-barbaric carving as the Gorgon and the Lion. At Trier or Metz or Arlon or Sens the sculptures are consistently classical in style and feeling, and the value of this fact is none the less if (with some writers) we find special geographical reasons for the occurrence of certain of these sculptures.[1] Smaller objects tell much the same tale. In particular the bronze 'fibulae' of Roman Britain are peculiarly British. Their commonest varieties are derived from Celtic prototypes and hardly occur abroad. The most striking example of this is supplied by the enamelled 'dragon-brooches'. Both their design (Fig. 19) and their gorgeous colouring are Celtic in spirit; they occur not seldom in Britain; on the Continent only four instances have been recorded.[2] Here certainly Roman Britain is more Celtic than Gallia Belgica or the Rhine Valley. Yet a complete survey of the brooches used in Roman Britain would show a large number of types which were equally common in Britain and on the Continent. Exceptions are always more interesting than rules—even in grammar. But the exceptions pass and the rules remain. The Castor ware and the Gorgon's head are exceptions. The rule stands that the material civilization of Britain was Roman. Except the Gorgon, every worked or sculptured stone at Bath follows the classical conventions. Except the Castor and New Forest pottery, all the better earthenware in use in Britain obeys the same law. The kind that was most generally employed for all but the meaner purposes, was not Castor but Samian or *terra sigillata*.[3] This ware is singularly characteristic of Roman-provincial art. As I have said above, it is copied wholesale from Italian originals. It is purely imitative and conventional; it reveals none of that delight in ornament, that spontaneousness in devising decoration and in working out artistic patterns which can clearly be traced in Late Celtic work. It is simply classical, in an inferior degree.

[Footnote 1: Michaelis, Loeschke and others assume an early intercourse between the Mosel basin and eastern Europe, and thereby explain both a statue in Pergamene style which was found at Metz and appears to have been carved there and also the Neumagen sculptures. As all these pieces were pretty certainly produced in Roman times, the early intercourse seems an inadequate cause. Moreover, Pergamene work, while rare in Italy, occurs in Aquitania and Africa, and may have been popular in the provinces.]

[Footnote 2: I have given a list in *Archaeologia Aeliana*, 1909, p. 420, to which four English and one foreign example have now to be added. See also Curle, *Newstead*, p. 319, and R.A. Smith, *Proc. Soc. Ant. Lond.*, xxii. 61.]

[Footnote 3: I may record here a protest against the attempts made from time to time to dispossess the term 'Samian'. Nothing better has been suggested in its stead, and the word itself has the merit of perfect lucidity. Of the various substitutes suggested, 'Pseudo-Arretine' is clumsy, 'Terra Sigillata' is at least as incorrect, and 'Gaulish' covers only a part of the field (*Proc. Soc. Antiq. Lond.*, xxiii. 120).]

[Illustration: FIG. 19. 'DRAGON-BROOCHES' FOUND AT CORBRIDGE (1/1). (P. 44.)]

The contrast between this Romano-British civilization and the native culture which preceded it can readily be seen if we compare for a moment a Celtic village and a Romano-British village. Examples of each have been excavated in the south-west of England, hardly thirty miles apart. The Celtic village is close to Glastonbury in Somerset. Of itself it is a small, poor place—just a group of pile dwellings rising out of a marsh, or (as it may then have been) a lake, and dating from the two centuries immediately preceding the Christian era.[1] Yet, poor as it was, its art is distinct. There one recognizes all that general delight in decoration and that genuine artistic instinct which mark Late Celtic work, while the technical details of the ornament, as, for example, the returning spiral, reveal their affinity with the same native fashion. On the other hand, no trace of classical workmanship or design intrudes. There has not been found anywhere in the village even a *fibula* with a hinge instead of a spring, or of an Italian (as opposed to a Late Celtic) pattern. Turn now to the Romano-British villages excavated by General Pitt-Rivers at Woodcuts and Rotherley and Woodyates, eleven miles south-west of Salisbury, near the Roman road from Old Sarum (Sorbiodunum) to Dorchester in Dorset.[2] Here you may search in vain for vestiges of the native art or of that delight in artistic ornament which characterizes it. Everywhere the monotonous Roman culture meets the eye. To pass from Glastonbury to Woodcuts is like passing from some old timbered village of Kent or Sussex to the uniform streets of a modern city suburb. Life at Woodcuts had, no doubt, its barbaric side. One writer who has discussed its character with a view to the present problem[3] comments, with evident distaste, on 'dwellings connected with pits used as storage rooms, refuse sinks, and burial places' and 'corpses crouching in un-Roman positions'. The first feature is not without its parallels in modern countries and it was doubtless common in ancient Italy. The second would be more significant if such skeletons occupied all or even the majority of the graves in these villages. Neither feature really mars the broad result, that the material life was Roman. Perhaps the villagers knew little enough of the Roman civilization in its higher aspects. Perhaps they did not speak Latin fluently or habitually. They may well have counted among the less Romanized of the southern Britons. Yet round them too hung the heavy inevitable atmosphere of the Roman material civilization.

[Footnote 1: The Glastonbury village was excavated in and after 1892 at intervals; a full account of the finds is now being issued by Bulleid and Gray (*The Glastonbury Lake Village*, vol. i, 1911), with a preface by Dr. R. Munro. The finds themselves are mostly at Glastonbury.]

[Footnote 2: Described in four quarto volumes, *Excavations in Cranborne Chase, &c.*, issued privately by the late General Pitt-Rivers, 1887-98.]

[Footnote 3: Vinogradoff, *Growth of the Manor*, p. 39. A parallel to the non-Roman burials found by General Pitt-Rivers may be found in the will of a Lingonian Gaul who died probably in the latter part of the first century. Apparently he was a Roman citizen, and his will is drawn in strict Roman fashion. But its last clause orders the burning of all his hunting apparatus, spears and nets, &c., on his funeral pyre, and thus betrays the Gaulish habit (Bruns, p. 308, ed. 1909).]

The facts which I have tried to set forth in the preceding paragraphs seem to me to possess more weight than is always allowed. Some writers, for instance M. Loth, speak as if the external environment of daily life, the furniture and decorations and architecture of our houses, or the clothes and buckles and brooches of our dress, bore no relation to the feelings and sentiments of those that used them. That is not a tenable proposition. The external fabric of life is not a negligible quantity but a real factor. On the one hand, it is hardly credible that an unromanized folk should adopt so much of Roman things as the British did, and yet remain uninfluenced. And it is equally incredible that, while it remained unromanized, it should either care or understand how to borrow all the externals of Roman life. The truth of this was clear to Tacitus in the days when the Romanization of Britain was proceeding. It may be recognized in the east or in Africa to-day. Even among the civilized nations of the present age the recent growth of stronger national feelings has been accompanied by a preference for home-products and home-manufactures and a distaste for foreign surroundings.

CHAPTER VI

ROMANIZATION IN THE LOCAL GOVERNMENT AND LAND-SYSTEM

I have dealt with the language and the material civilization of the province of Britain. I pass to a third and harder question, the administrative and legal framework of local Romano-British life. Here we have to discuss the extent to which the Roman town-system of the *colonia* and *municipium*, and the Roman land-system of the *villa* penetrated Britain. And, first, as to the towns. Britain, we know, contained five municipalities of the privileged Italian type. The *colonia* of Camulodunum (Colchester) and the *municipium* of Verulamium (St. Albans), both in the south-east of the island, were established soon after the Claudian conquest. The *colonia* of Lindum (Lincoln) was probably founded in the early Flavian period (A.D. 70-80), when the Ninth Legion, hitherto at Lincoln, was probably pushed forward to York. The *colonia* at Glevum (Gloucester) arose in A.D. 96-98, as an inscription seems definitely to attest. Lastly, the *colonia* at Eburacum (York) must have grown up during the second or the early third century, under the ramparts of the legionary fortress, though separated from it by the intervening river Ouse.[1] Each of these five towns had, doubtless, its dependent *ager attributus*, which may have been as large as an average English county, and each provided the local government for its territory.[2] That implies a definitely Roman form of local government for a considerable area—a larger area, certainly, than received such organization in northern Gaul. Yet it accounts, on the most liberal estimate, for barely one-eighth of the civilized part of the province.

[Footnote 1: The fortress was situated on the left or east bank of the Ouse close to the present cathedral, which stands wholly within its area. Parts of the Roman walls can still be traced, especially at the so-called Multangular Tower. The municipality lay on the other (west) bank of the Ouse, near the railway station, where various mosaics indicate dwelling-houses. Its outline and plan are, however, not known. Even its situation has not been generally recognized.]

[Footnote 2: If the evidence of milestones may be pressed, the 'territory' of Eburacum extended southwards at least twenty miles to Castleford, and that of Lincoln at least fourteen miles to Littleborough (*Ephemeris Epigraphica*, vii. 1105=ix. 1253, where the last two lines are AVGG EB | MP XX (or XXII), and vii. 1097). The general size of these municipal 'territoria' is amply proved by Continental inscriptions.]

Of the rest, some part may have been included in the Imperial Domains, which covered wide tracts in every province and were administered for local purposes by special procurators of the Emperor. The lead-mining districts—

Mendip in Somerset, the neighbourhood of Matlock in Derbyshire, the Shelve Hills west of Wroxeter, the Halkyn region in Flintshire, the moors of south-west Yorkshire—must have belonged to these Domains, and for the most part are actually attested by inscriptions on lead-pigs as Imperial property. Of other domain lands we meet one early instance at Silchester in the reign of Nero[1]—perhaps the confiscated estates of some British prince or noble—and though we have no further direct evidence, the analogy of other provinces suggests that the area increased as the years went by. Yet it is likely that in Britain, as indeed in Gaul,[2] the domain lands were comparatively small in amount. Like the municipalities, they account only for a part of the province.

[Footnote 1: Tile inscribed NERCLCAEAVGGER, *Nero Claudius Caesar Augustus Germanicus* (*Eph*. ix. 1267). It differs markedly from the ordinary tiles found at Silchester, and plainly belongs to a different period in the history of the site. Possibly the estate, or whatever it was, did not remain Imperial after Nero's downfall; compare Plutarch, *Galba*, 5. The Combe Down *Principia* (C. vii. 62), which are certainly not military, may supply another example, of about A.D. 210 (*Vict. Hist. Somerset*, i. 311; *Eph*. ix. p. 516).]

[Footnote 2: Hirschfeld in Lehmann's *Beiträge zur alten Geschichte*, ii. 307, 308. Much of the Gaulish domain land appears to date from confiscations in A.D. 197.]

Throughout all the rest of the British province, or at least of its civilized area, the local government was probably organized on the same cantonal system as obtained in northern Gaul. According to this system the local unit was the former territory of the tribe or canton, and the local magistrates were the chiefs or nobles of the tribe. That may appear at first sight to be a native system, wholly out of harmony with the Roman method of government by municipalities. Yet such was not its actual effect. The cantonal or tribal magistrates were classified and arranged just like the magistrates of a municipality. They even used the same titles. The cantonal *civitas* had its *duoviri* and quaestors and so forth, and its *ordo* or senate, precisely like any municipal *colonia* or *municipium*. So far from wearing a native aspect, this cantonal system merely became one of the influences which aided the Romanization of the country. It did not, indeed, involve, like the municipal system, the substitution of an Italian for a native institution. Instead, it permitted the complete remodelling of the native institution by the interpenetration of Italian influences.

We can discern the cantonal system at several points in Britain. But the British cantons were smaller and less wealthy than those of Gaul, and therefore they have not left their mark, either in monuments or in nomenclature, so clearly as we might desire. Many inscriptions record the working of the system in Gaul. Many modern towns—Paris, Reims, Chartres, and thirty or forty others—derive their present names from those of the ancient cantons, and not from those of the ancient towns. In Britain we find only one such inscription (Fig. 15),[1] only one town called in antiquity by a tribal name—and that a doubtful instance[2]—and no single case of a modern town-name which is derived from the name of a tribe.[3] We have, however, some curious evidence from another source. There is a late and obscure *Geography of the Roman Empire* which was probably written at Ravenna somewhere about A.D. 700, and which, as its author's name is lost, is generally quoted as the work of 'Ravennas'. It consists for the most part of mere lists of names, about which it adds very few details. But in the case of Britain it notes the municipal rank of the various *coloniae*, and it further appends tribal names to nine or ten town-names, which are thus distinguished from all other British place-names. For example, we have Venta Belgarum (Winchester), not Venta simply; Corinium Dobunorum (Cirencester), not Corinium simply. The towns thus specially marked out are just those towns which are also declared by their actual remains to have been the chief country towns of Roman Britain. This coincidence can hardly be an accident. We may infer that the towns to which the Ravennas appends tribal names were the cantonal capitals of the districts of Roman Britain, and that a list of them, perhaps mutilated and imperfect, has been preserved by some chance in this late writer. In other words, the larger part of Roman Britain was divided up into districts corresponding to the territories of the Celtic tribes; each had its capital, and presumably its magistrates and senate, as the above-mentioned inscription shows that the Silures had at Venta Silurum. We may suppose, indeed, that the district magistrates—the county council, as it would now be called—were also the magistrates of the country town. The same cantonal system, then, existed here as in northern Gaul. Only, it was weaker in Britain. It could not impose tribal names on the towns, and it went down easily when the Empire fell. In Gaul, Lutetia Parisiorum became Parisiis and is now Paris, and Nemetacum Atrebatum became Atrebatis and is now Arras. In Britain, Calleva Atrebatum (Silchester) remained Calleva, so far as we know, till it perished altogether in the fifth century.[4]

[Footnote 1: Found at Venta Silurum (Caerwent) in 1903: ... *leg. legi[i] Aug. proconsul(i) provinc. Narbonensis, leg. Aug. pr. pr. provi. Lugudunen(sis): ex decreto ordinis respubl(ica) civit(atis) Silurum*—a monument erected by the cantonal senate of the Silures to some general of the Second legion at Isca Silurum, twelve miles from Caerwent—perhaps to Claudius Paulinus, early in third century (*Athenaeum*, Sept. 26, 1903; *Archaeologia*, lix. 120; *Eph.* ix. 1012). Other inscriptions mention a *civis Cantius*, a *civitas Catuvellaunorum* and the like, but their evidence is less distinct.]

[Illustration: FIG. 20. INSCRIPTION FOUND AT CAERWENT (VENTA SILURUM) MENTIONING A DECREE OF THE SENATE OF THE CANTON OF SILURES.]

[Footnote 2: *Icinos* in *Itin. Ant.* 474. 6 may well be Venta Icenorum (*Victoria Hist. of Norfolk*, i. 286, 300).]

[Footnote 3: Canterbury may seem an exception. But its name comes ultimately from the Early English form of Cantium, not from the Cantii. In the south-west and in Wales, tribal names like Dumnonii (Devonshire), Demetae, Ordovices, have lingered on in one form or another, and, according to Professor Rhys, Bernicia is derivable from Brigantes. But these cases differ widely from the Gaulish instances.]

[Footnote 4: Ravennas (ed. Parthey and Pinder), pp. 425 foll. I have given a list of the towns in my Appendix to Mommsen's *Provinces of the Empire* (English trans., 1909), ii. 352.]

Of the smaller local organizations, little can be said. Towns existed, but many of them were the tribal capitals mentioned in the last paragraph, and these, as I have said, were doubtless ruled by the magistrates of the tribes. It is idle to guess who administered the towns that were not such capitals or who controlled the various villages scattered through the country. Nor can we pretend to know much more about the size and character of the estates which corresponded to the country-houses and farms of which remains survive. The 'villa' system of demesne farms and serfs or *coloni*[1] which obtained elsewhere was doubtless familiar in Britain; indeed, the Theodosian Code definitely refers to British *coloni*.[2] But whether it was the only rural system in Britain is beyond proof, and previous attempts to work out the problem have done little more than demonstrate the fact.[3] It is quite possible that here, or indeed in any province, other forms of estates and of land tenure may have existed beside the predominant villa.[4] The one thing needed is evidence. And in any case the net result appears fairly certain. The bulk of British local government must have been carried on through Roman municipalities, through imperial estates, and still more through tribal *civitates* using a Romanized constitution. The bulk of the landed estates must have conformed in their legal aspects to the 'villas' of other provinces. Whatever room there may be for survival of native customs or institutions, we have no evidence that they survived, within the Romanized area, either in great amount or in any form which contrasted with the general Roman character of the country.

[Footnote 1: The term 'villa' is generally used to denote Romano-British country-houses and farms, irrespective of their legal classification. The use is so firmly established, both in England and abroad, that it would be idle to attempt to alter it. But for clearness I have thought it better in this paper to employ the term 'villa' only where I refer to the definite 'villa' system.]

[Footnote 2: Cod. Theod. xi. 7.2.]

[Footnote 3: For instance, Mr. Seebohm (*English Village Community*, pp. 254 foll.) connects the suffix 'ham' with the Roman 'villa' and apparently argues that the occurrence of the suffix indicates in general the former existence of a 'villa'. But his map showing the percentage of local names ending in 'ham' in various counties disproves his view completely. For the distribution of the suffix 'ham' and the frequency of Roman country-houses and farms do not coincide. In Norfolk, for instance, 'ham' is common, but there is hardly a trace of a Roman country-house or farm in the whole county (*Victoria Hist. of Norfolk*, i. 294-8). Somerset, on the other hand, is crowded with Roman country-houses, and has hardly any 'hams'.]

[Footnote 4: Professor Vinogradoff, *Growth of the Manor* (chap. ii), argues strongly for the existence of Celtic land-tenures besides the Roman 'villa' system. 'There was room (he suggests) for all sorts of conditions, from almost exact copies of Roman municipal corporations and Italian country-houses to tribal arrangements scarcely coloured by a thin sprinkling of imperial administration' (p. 83). As will be seen, this is not improbable. But I can find no definite proof of it. If northern Gaul were better known to us, it might provide a decisive analogy. But the Gaulish evidence itself seems at present disputable.]

CHAPTER VII

CHRONOLOGY OF THE ROMANIZATION

From this consideration of the evidence available to illustrate the Romanization of Britain, I pass to the inquiry how far history helps us to trace out the chronology of the process. A few facts and probabilities emerge as guides. Intercourse between south-eastern Britain and the Roman world had already begun before the Roman conquest in A.D. 43. Latin words, as I have said above (p. 24), had begun to appear on the native British coinage, and Arretine pottery had found its way to such places as Foxton in Cambridgeshire, Alchester in Oxfordshire, and Southwark in Surrey.[1] The establishment of a *municipium* at Verulamium (St. Albans) sometime before A.D. 60, and probably even before A.D. 50,[2] points the same way. The peculiar status of *municipium* was granted in the early Empire especially to native provincial towns which had become Romanized without official Roman action or settlement of Roman soldiers or citizens, and which had, as it were, merited municipal privileges. It is quite likely that such Romanization had begun at Verulam before the Roman conquest, and formed the justification for the early grant of such privileges. Certainly the whole lowland area, as far west as Exeter and Shrewsbury, and as far north as the Humber, was conquered before Claudius died, and Romanization may have commenced in it at once.

[Footnote 1: Babington, *Anc. Cambridgeshire*, p. 64; E. Krüger, *Westd. Korr.-Blatt*, 1904, p. 181; my note, *Proc. Soc. Antiq. Lond.*, xxi. 461 *Journal of Roman Studies*, i. 146. Mr. H.B. Walters has dealt with the Southwark piece in the *Proceedings of the Cambridge Antiq. Society*, xii. 107, but with some errors. The Alchester piece may be later than A.D. 43.]

[Footnote 2: The grant is very much more likely to have been made by Claudius than by Nero, and more likely to belong to the earlier than to the later years of Claudius.]

Thirty years later Agricola, who was obviously a better administrator than a general, openly encouraged the process. According to Tacitus, his efforts met with great success; Latin began to be spoken, the toga to be worn, temples, town halls, and private houses to be built in Roman fashion.[1] Agricola appears to have been merely carrying out the policy of his age. Certainly it is just at this period (about 75-85 A.D.) that towns like Silchester, Bath, Caerwent, seem to take definite shape,[2] and civil judges (*legati iuridici*) were appointed, presumably to administer the justice more frequently required by the advancing civilization.[3] In A.D. 85 it was thought safe to reduce the garrison by a legion and some auxiliaries.[4] Progress, however, was not maintained. About 115-20, and again about 155-63 and 175-80, the northern part of the province was vexed by serious risings, and the civilian area was doubtless kept somewhat in disturbance.[5] Probably it was at some point in this period that the flourishing country town of Isurium (Aldborough), fifteen miles from York, had to shield itself by a stone wall and ditch.[6]

[Footnote 1: Tac. *Agr.* 21, quoted in note 3 to p. 13.]

[Footnote 2: Silchester was plainly laid out in Roman fashion all at once on a definite street plan, and though some few of its houses may be older, the town as a whole seems to have taken its rise from this event. The evidence of coins implies that the development of the place began in the Flavian period (*Athenaeum*, Dec. 15, 1904). At Bath the earliest datable stones belong to the same time (*Victoria Hist. of Somerset*, vol. i, Roman Bath), the first being a fragmentary inscription of A.D. 76. At Caerwent the evidence is confined to coins and fibulae, none of which seem earlier than Vespasian or Domitian: for the coins see *Clifton Antiq. Club's Proceedings*, v. 170-82.]

[Footnote 3: A. von Domaszewski, *Rhein. Mus.*, xlvi. 599; C. ix. 5533 (as completed by Domaszewski), inscription of Salvius Liberalis; C. iii. 2864=9960, inscription of Iavolenus Priscus. Both these belong to the Flavian period. Other instances are known from the second century.]

[Footnote 4: *Classical Review*, xviii. (1904) 458; xix. (1905) 58, withdrawal of Batavian cohorts. The withdrawal of *Legio ii Adiutrix* is well known.]

[Footnote 5: See my papers in *Archaeologia Aeliana*, xxv. (1904) 142-7, and *Proceedings of Soc. of Antiq. of Scotland*, xxxviii. 454.]

[Footnote 6: The town wall of Isurium, partly visible to-day in Mr. A.S. Lawson's garden, is constructed in a fashion which suggests rather the second century than the later date when most of the town walls in Britain and Gaul were probably built, the end of the third or even the fourth century. Thus, its stones show the 'diamond broaching' which occurs on the Vallum of Pius, and which must therefore have been in use during the second century.]

Peace hardly set in till the opening of the third century. It was then, I think, that country-houses and farms first became common in all parts of the civilized area. The statistics of datable objects discovered in these buildings seem conclusive on this point. Except in Kent and the south-eastern region generally, not only coins, but also pottery of the first century are infrequent, and many sites have yielded nothing earlier than about A.D. 250. Despite the ill name that attaches to the third and fourth centuries, they were perhaps for Britain, as for parts of Gaul,[1] a period of progressive prosperity. Certainly, the number of British country-houses and farms inhabited during the years A.D. 280-350 must have been very large. Prosperity culminated, perhaps, in the Constantinian Age. Then, as Eumenius tells us, skilled artisans abounded in Britain far more than in Gaul, and were fetched from the island to build public and private edifices as far south as Autun.[2] Then also, and, indeed, as late as 360, British corn was largely exported to the Rhine Valley,[3] and British cloth earned a notice in the eastern Edict of Diocletian.[4] The province at that time was a prosperous and civilized region, where Latin speech and culture might be expected to prevail widely.

[Footnote 1: Mommsen, *Röm. Gesch.*, v. 97, 106, and Ausonius, *passim.*]

[Footnote 2: Eumenius, *Paneg. Constantio Caesari*, 21 *civitas Aeduorum ... plurimos quibus illae provinciae* (Britain) *redundabant accepit artifices, et nunc exstructione veterum domorum et refectione operum publicorum et templorum instauratione consurgit.*]

[Footnote 3: Ammianus, xviii. 2,3, *annona a Brittaniis sueta transferri*; Zosimus, iii. 5.]

[Footnote 4: Edict. Diocl. xix. 36. Compare Eumenius, *Paneg. Constantino Aug.*, 9 *pecorum innumerabilis multitudo ... onusta velleribus*, and *Constantio Caesari*, 11 *tanto laeta munere pastionum*. Traces of dyeing works have been discovered at Silchester (*Archaeologia*, liv. 460, &c.) and of fulling in rural dwellings at Chedworth in Gloucestershire, Darenth in Kent, and Titsey in Surrey (Fox, *Archaeologia*, lix. 207).]

No golden age lasts long. Before 350, probably in 343, Constans had to cross the Channel and repel the Picts and other assailants.[1] After 368 such aid was more often and more urgently required. Significantly enough, the lists of coins found in some country-houses close about 350-60, while others remained occupied till about 385 or even later. The rural districts, it is plain, began then to be no longer safe; some houses were burnt by marauding bands, and some abandoned by their owners.[2] Therewith came necessarily, as in many other provinces, a decline of Roman influences and a rise of barbarism. Men took the lead who were not polished and civilized Romans of Italy or of the provinces, but warriors and captains of warrior bands. The Menapian Carausius, whatever his birthplace,[3] was the forerunner of a numerous class. Finally, the great raid of 406-7 and its sequel severed Britain from Rome. A wedge of barbarism was driven in between the two, and the central government, itself in bitter need, ceased to send officers to rule the province and to command its troops. Britain was left to itself. Yet even now it did not seek separation from Rome. All that we know supports the view of Mommsen. It was not Britain which broke loose from the Empire, but the Empire which gave up Britain.[4]

[Footnote 1: Ammianus, xx. 1. The expedition was important enough to be recorded—unless I am mistaken—on coins such as those which show victorious Constans on a galley, recrossing the Channel after his success

- 34 -

[(Cohen, 9-13, &c.). On the history of the whole period for Britain see *Cambridge Medieval History*, i. 378, 379.]

[Footnote 2: See, for example, the coin-finds of the country-houses at Thruxton, Abbots Ann, Clanville, Holbury, Carisbrooke, &c., in Hampshire (*Victoria Hist. of Hants*, i. 294 foll.). The Croydon hoard deposited about A.D. 351 (*Numismatic Chronicle*, 1905, p. 37) may be assigned to the same cause.]

[Footnote 3: It is hard to believe him an Irishman, though Professor Rhys supports the idea (*Cambrian Archaeol. Assoc., Kerry Meeting*, 1891). The one ancient authority, Aurelius Victor (xxxix. 20), describes him simply as *Menapiae civis*. The Gaulish Menapii were well known; the Irish Menapii were very obscure, and the brief reference can only refer to the former.]

[Footnote 4: Mommsen, *Röm. Gesch.*, v. 177. Zosimus, vi. 5 (A.D. 408), in a puzzling passage describes Britain as revolting from Rome when Constantine was tyrant (A.D. 407-11). It is generally assumed that when Constantine failed to protect these regions, they set up for themselves, and in that troubled time such a step would be natural enough. But Zosimus, a little later on (vi. 10, A.D. 410), casually states that Honorius wrote to Britain, bidding the provincials defend themselves, so that the act of 408 cannot have been final—unless, indeed, as the context of Zosimus suggests and as Gothofredus and others have thought, the name 'Britain' is here a copyist's mistake for 'Bruttii' or some other Italian name. In any case the 'groans of the Britons' recorded by Gildas show that the island looked to Rome long after 410. On Constantine see Freeman, *Western Europe in the Fifth Century*, pp. 48, 148 and Bury, *Life of St. Patrick*, p. 329.]

Such is, in brief, the positive evidence, archaeological, linguistic, and historical, which illustrates the Romanization of Britain. The conclusions which it allows seem to be two. First, and mainly: the Empire did its work in our island as it did generally on the western continent. It Romanized the province, introducing Roman speech and thought and culture. Secondly, this Romanization was perhaps not uniform throughout all sections of the population. Within the lowlands the result was on the whole achieved. In the towns and among the upper class in the country Romanization was substantially complete—as complete as in northern Gaul, and possibly indeed even more complete. But both the lack of definite evidence and the probabilities of the case require us to admit that the peasantry may have been less thoroughly Romanized. It was covered with a superimposed layer of Roman civilization. But beneath this layer the native element may have remained potentially, if not actually, Celtic, and in the remoter districts the native speech may have lingered on, like Erse or Manx to-day, as a rival to the more fashionable Latin. How far this happened actually within the civilized lowland area we cannot tell. But we may be sure that the military region, Wales and the north, never became thoroughly Romanized, and Cornwall and western Devon also lie beyond the pale (p. 21). Here the Britons must have remained Celtic, or at least capable of a reversion to the Celtic tradition. Here, at any rate, a Celtic revival was possible.

CHAPTER VIII

THE SEQUEL, THE CELTIC REVIVAL IN THE LATER EMPIRE

So far we have considered the province of Britain as it was while it still remained in real fact a province. Let us now turn to the sequel and ask how it fits in with its antecedents. The Romanization, we find, held its own for a while. The sense of belonging to the Empire had not quite died out even in sixth-century Britain. Roman names continued to be used, not exclusively but freely enough, by Britons. Roman 'culture words' seem to occur in the later British language, and some at least of these may be traceable to the Roman occupation of the island. Roman military terms appear, if scantily. Roman inscriptions are occasionally set up. The Romanization of Britain was plainly no mere interlude, which passed without leaving a mark behind.[1] But it was crossed by two hostile forges, a Celtic revival and an English invasion.

[Footnote 1: Much of the ornamentation used by post-Roman Celtic art comes from Roman sources, in particular the interlaced or plaitwork, which has been well studied by Mr. Romilly Allen. But how far it was borrowed from Romano-British originals and how far from similar Roman-provincial work on the Continent, is not very clear. (See p. 36.)]

The Celtic revival was due to many influences. We may find one cause for it in the Celtic environment of the province. After 407 the Romanized area was cut off from Rome. Its nearest neighbours were now the less-Romanized Britons of districts like Cornwall and the foreign Celts of Ireland and the north. These were weighty influences in favour of a Celtic revival. And they were all the more potent because, in or even before the period under discussion, the opening of the fifth century, a Celtic migration seems to have set in from the Irish coasts. The details of this migration are unknown, and the few traces which survive of it are faint and not altogether intelligible. The principal movement was that of the Scotti from North Ireland into Caledonia, with the result that, once settled there, or perhaps rather in the course of settling there, they went on to pillage Roman Britain. There were also movements in the south, but apparently on a smaller scale and a more peaceful plan.[1] At a date given commonly as A.D. 265-70—though there does not seem to be any very good reason for it—the Dessi or Déisi were expelled from Meath and a part of them settled in the south-west of Wales, in the land then called Demetia. This was a region which was both thinly inhabited and imperfectly Romanized. In it fugitives from Ireland might easily find room. The settlement may have been formed, as Professor Bury suggests, with the consent of the Imperial Government and under conditions of service. But we are entirely ignorant whether these exiles from Ireland numbered tens or scores or hundreds, and this uncertainty renders speculation dangerous. If the newcomers were few and their new homes were in the remote west beyond Carmarthen (Maridunum), formal consent would hardly have been required. Other Irish immigrants probably followed. Their settlements were apparently confined to Cornwall and the south-west coast of Wales, and their influence may easily be overrated. Some, indeed, came as enemies, though perhaps rather as enemies to the Roman than to the Celtic elements in the province. Such must have been Niall of the Nine Hostages, who was killed—according to the traditional chronology—about A.D. 405 on the British coast and perhaps in the Channel itself.

[Footnote 1: Professor Rhys, *Cambrian Archaeol. Assoc. Kerry Meeting*, 1891, and *Celtic Britain* (ed. 3, 1904, p. 247), is inclined to minimize the invasions of southern Britain (Cornwall and Wales). Professor Bury (*Life of St. Patrick*, p. 288) tends to emphasize them; see also Zimmer, *Nennius Vindicatus*, pp. 84 foll., and Kuno Meyer, *Cymmrodorion Transactions*, 1895-6, pp. 55 foll. The decision of the question seems to depend upon whether we should regard the Goidelic elements visible in western Britain as due in part to an original Goidelic population or ascribe them wholly to Irish immigrants. At present philologists do not seem able to speak with certainty on this point. But the evidence for some amount of invasion seems adequate.]

All this must have contributed to the reintroduction of Celtic national feeling and culture. A Celtic immigrant, it may be, was the man who set up the Ogam pillar at Silchester (Fig. 21), which was discovered in the excavations of 1893.[1] The circumstances of the discovery show that this pillar belongs to the very latest period in the history of Calleva. Its inscription is Goidelic: that is, it does not belong to the ordinary Callevan population, which was presumably Brythonic. It may be best explained as the work of some western Celt who reached Silchester before its British citizens abandoned it in despair. We do not know the date of that event, though we may conjecturally put it before, and perhaps a good many years before, A.D. 500. In any case, an Ogam monument had been set up before it occurred, and the presence of such an object would seem to prove that Celtic things had made their way even into this eastern Romanized town.

[Footnote 1: *Archaeologia*, liv. 233, 441; Rhys and Brynmor Jones, *Welsh People*, pp. 45, 65; *Victoria Hist. of Hampshire*, i. 279; *English Hist. Review*, xix. 628. Whether the man who wrote was Irish or British depends on the answer to the question set forth in the preceding note. Unfortunately, we do not know when the Ogam script came first into use. Professor Rhys tells me that the Silchester example may quite conceivably belong to the fifth century.]

[Illustration: FIG. 21. OGAM INSCRIPTION FROM SILCHESTER.]

But a more powerful aid to the revival may be found in another fact—that is the destruction of the Romanized part of Britain by the invading Saxons. War, and especially defensive war against invaders, must always weaken the higher forms of any country's civilization. Here the agony was long, and the assailants cruel and powerful, and the country itself was somewhat weak. Its wealth was easily exhausted. Its towns were small. Its fortresses were not impregnable. Its leaders were divided and disloyal. Moreover, the assault fell on the very parts of Britain which were the seats of Roman culture. Even in the early years of the fourth century it had been found necessary to defend the coasts of East Anglia, Kent, and Sussex, some of the most thickly populated and highly civilized parts of Britain, against the pirates by a series of forts which extended from the Wash to Spithead, and were known as the forts of the Saxon Shore. Fifty or seventy years later the raiders, whether English seamen or Picts and Scots from Caledonia and Ireland, devastated the coasts of the province and perhaps reached even the midlands.[1] When, seventy years later still, the English came, no longer to plunder but to settle, they occupied first the Romanized area of the island. As the Romano-Britons retired from the south and east, as Silchester was evacuated in despair[2] and Bath and Wroxeter were stormed and left desolate, the very centres of Romanized life were extinguished. Not a single one remained an inhabited town. Destruction fell even on Canterbury, where the legends tell of intercourse between Briton or Saxon, and on London, where ecclesiastical writers fondly place fifth- and sixth-century bishops. Both sites lay empty and untenanted for many years. Only in the far west, at Exeter or at Caerwent, does our evidence allow us to guess at a continuing Romano-British life.

[Footnote 1: About A.D. 405 Patrick was carried off from Bannavem Taberniae. If this represents the Romano-British village on Watling Street called Bannaventa, near Daventry in Northants (*Victoria Hist.* i. 186), the raids must have covered all the midlands: see *Engl. Hist. Review*, 1895, p. 711; Zimmer, *Realenc. für protestantische Theol.* x. (1901), Art. 'Keltische Kirche'; Bury, *Life of St. Patrick*, p. 322. There are, however, too many uncertainties surrounding this question to let us derive much help from it.]

[Footnote 2: *Engl. Hist. Review*, xix. 625; Fox, *Victoria Hist. of Hampshire*, i. 371-2.]

The same destruction came also on the population. During the long series of disasters, many of the Romanized inhabitants of the lowland regions must have perished. Many must have fallen into slavery, and may have been sold into foreign lands. The remnant, such as it was, doubtless retired to the west. But, in doing so, it exchanged the region of walled cities and civilized houses, of city life and Roman culture, for a Celtic land. No doubt it attempted to keep up its Roman fashions. The writers may well be correct who speak of two conflicting parties, Roman and Celtic, among the Britons of the sixth century. But the Celtic element triumphed. Gildas, about A.D. 540, describes a Britain confined to the west of our island, which is very largely Celtic and not Roman.[1] Had the English invaded the island from the Atlantic, we might have seen a different spectacle. The Celtic element would have perished utterly: the Roman would have survived. As it was, the attack fell on the east and south of the island—that is, on the lowlands of Britain. Safe in its western hills, the Celtic revival had full course.

[Footnote 1: How much of Britain was still British when Gildas wrote, he does not tell us. But he mentions only the extreme west (Damnonii, Demetae); his general atmosphere is Celtic, and his rhetoric contains no references to a flourishing civilization. We may conclude that the Romanized part of Britain had been lost by his time, or that, if some part was still held by the British, long war had destroyed its civilization. Unfortunately we cannot trust the traditional English chronology of the period. As to the date of Gildas, cf. W.H. Stevenson, *Academy*, October 26, 1895, &c.; I see no reason to put either Gildas or any part of the *Epistula* later than about 540.]

It is this Celtic revival which can best explain the history of Britannia minor, Brittany across the seas in the western extremity of Gaul. How far this region had been Romanized during the first four centuries seems uncertain. Towns were scarce in it, and country-houses, though not altogether infrequent or insignificant, were unevenly distributed. At some period not precisely known, perhaps in the first half or the middle of the third century, it was in open rebellion, and the commander of the Sixth Legion (at York), one Artorius Justus, was sent with a part of the British garrison to reduce it to obedience.[1] It may therefore have been, as Mommsen suggests, one of the least Romanized corners of Gaul, and in it the native idiom may have retained unusual vitality. Yet that native speech was not strong enough to live on permanently. The Celtic which is spoken to-day in Brittany is not a Gaulish but a British Celtic; it is the result of British influences. Brittany would have sooner or later become assimilated to the general Romano-Gaulish civilization, had not its Celtic elements won fresh strength from immigrant Britons. This immigration is usually described as an influx of refugees fleeing from Britain before the English advance. That, no doubt, was one side of it. But the principal immigrants, so far as we know their names, came from Devon and Cornwall,[2] and some certainly did not come as fugitives. The King Riotamus who (as Jordanes tells us) brought 12,000 Britons in A.D. 470 to aid the Roman cause in Gaul, was plainly not seeking shelter from the English.[3] We must connect him, and indeed the whole fifth-century movement of Britons into Gaul, with the Celtic revival and with the same causes that produced for instance, the Scotic invasion of Caledonia.

[Footnote 1: C. iii. 1919=Dessau 2770. The inscription must be later than (about) A.D. 200, and it somewhat resembles another inscription (C. iii. 3228) of the reign of Gallienus, which mentions *milites vexill. leg. Germanicar. et Britannicin. cum auxiliis earum.* Presumably it is either earlier than the Gallic Empire of 258-73, or falls between that and the revolt of Carausius in 287. The notion of O. Fiebiger (*De classium Italicarum historia,* in *Leipziger Studien,* xv. 304) that it belongs to the Aremoric revolts of the fifth century is, I think, wrong. Such an expedition from Britain at such a date is incredible.]

[Footnote 2: The attempt to find eastern British names in Brittany seems a failure. M. de la Borderie, for instance, thinks that Corisopitum (or whatever the exact form of the name is) was colonized from Corstopitum (Corbridge on the Tyne, near Hadrian's Wall). But the latter, always to some extent a military site, can hardly have sent out ordinary *émigrés,* while the former has hardly an historical existence at all, and may be an ancient error for *civitas Coriosolitum* (C. xiii (I), i. p. 491).]

[Footnote 3: Freeman (*Western Europe in the Fifth Century,* p. 164) suggests that a migration of Britons into Gaul had been in progress, perhaps since the days of Magnus Maximus, and that by 470 there was a regular British state on the Loire, from which Riotamus led his 12,000 men. Hodgkin (*Cornwall and Brittany,* Penryn, 1911) suggests that the soldiers of Maximus settled on the Loire about 388, and that Riotamus was one of their descendants. He quotes Gildas as saying that the British troops of Maximus went abroad with him and never returned. That, however, is an entirely different thing from saying that they settled in a definite part of Gaul. For this latter statement I can find no evidence, and the Celtic revival in our island seems to provide a better setting for the whole incident of Riotamus.

If Professor Bury is right (*Life of Patrick,* p. 354), Riotamus had a predecessor in Dathi, who is said to have gone from Ireland to Gaul about A.D. 428 to help the Romans and Aetius. Zimmer (*Nennius Vind.,* p. 85) rejects the tale. But it fits in well with the Celtic revival.]

This destruction of Romano-British life produced a curious result which would be difficult to explain if we could not assign it to this cause. There is a marked and unmistakable gap between the Romano-British and the Later Celtic periods. However numerous may be the Latin personal names and 'culture words' in Welsh, it is beyond question that the tradition of Roman days was lost in Britain during the fifth or early sixth century. That is seen plainly in the scanty literature of the age. Gildas wrote about A.D. 540, three generations after the Saxon settlements had begun. He was a priest, well educated, and well acquainted with Latin, which he once calls *nostra lingua.* He was also not unfriendly to the Roman party among the Britons, and not unaware of the relation of Britain to the Empire.[1] Yet he knew substantially nothing of the history of Britain as a Roman province. He drew from some source now lost to us—possibly an ecclesiastical or semi-ecclesiastical writer—some details of the persecution of Diocletian and of the career of Magnus Maximus.[2] For the rest, his ideas of Roman history may be judged by his statement that the two Walls which defended the north of the province—the Walls of Hadrian and Pius—were built somewhere between A.D. 388 and 440. He had some tradition of the coming of the English about 450, and of the reason why they came. But his knowledge of anything previous to that event was plainly most imperfect.

[Footnote 1: Mommsen, Preface to *Gildas* (Mon. Germ. Hist.), pp. 9-10. Gildas is, however, rather more Celtic in tone than Mommsen seems to allow. Such a phrase as *ita ut non Britannia sed Romania censeretur* implies a consciousness of contrast between Briton and Roman. Freeman (*Western Europe*, p. 155) puts the case too strongly the other way.]

[Footnote 2: Magnus Maximus, as the opponent of Theodosius, seems to have been damned by the Church writers. Compare the phrases of Orosius, vii. 35 (Theodosius) *posuit in Deo spem suam seseque adversus Maximum tyrannum sola fide maior proripuit* and *ineffabili iudicio Dei* and *Theodosius victoriam Deo procurante suscipit.*]

The *Historia Brittonum*, compiled a century or two later, preserves even less memory of things Roman. There is some hint of a *vetus traditio seniorum*. But the narrative which professes to be based on it bears little relation to the actual facts; the growth of legend is perceptible, and even those details that are borrowed from literary sources like Gildas, Jerome, Prosper, betray great ignorance on the part of the borrower.[1] On the other hand, the native Celtic instinct is more definitely alive and comes into sharper contrast with the idea of Rome. Throughout, no detail occurs which enlarges our knowledge of Roman or of early post-Roman Britain. The same features recur in later writers who might be or have been supposed to have had access to British sources. Geoffrey of Monmouth—to take only the most famous—asserts that he used a Breton book which told him all manner of facts otherwise unknown. The statement is by no means improbable. But, for all that, the pages of Geoffrey contain no new fact about the first five centuries which is also true.[2] From first to last, the Celtic tradition preserves no real remnant of recollections dating from the Romano-British age. Those who might have handed down such memories had either perished in wars with the English or sunk back into the native environment of the west.[3]

[Footnote 1: The story of Vortigern and Hengist now first occurs and is obvious tradition or legend. A prince with a Celtic name may have ruled Kent in 450. There were, indeed, plenty of rulers with barbaric names in the fourth and fifth centuries of the Empire. But the tale cannot be called certain history.]

[Footnote 2: Thus, he refers to Silchester, and so good a judge as Stubbs once suggested that for this he had some authority now lost to us. Yet the mere fact that Geoffrey knows only the English name Silchester disproves this idea. Had he used a genuinely ancient authority, he would have (as elsewhere) employed the Roman name. Another explanation may be given. Geoffrey wrote in an antiquarian age, when the ruins of Roman towns were being noted. Both he and Henry of Huntingdon seem to have heard of the Silchester ruins, and both accordingly inserted the place into their pages.]

[Footnote 3: The English mediaeval chronicles have sometimes been supposed to preserve facts otherwise forgotten about Roman times. So far as I can judge, this is not the case, even with Henry of Huntingdon. Henry, in the later editions of his work, borrowed a few facts from Geoffrey of Monmouth, which are wanting in his first edition (see the All Souls MS.; the truth is obscured in the Rolls Series text). He also preserves one local tradition from Colchester: otherwise he contains nothing which need puzzle any inquirer. Giraldus Cambrensis, when at Rome, saw some manuscript which contained a list of the five provinces of fourth-century Britain— otherwise unknown throughout the Middle Ages (*Archaeol. Oxoniensis*, 1894, p. 224).]

But we are moving in a dim land of doubts and shadows. He who wanders here, wanders at his peril, for certainties are few, and that which at one moment seems a fact, is only too likely, as the quest advances, to prove a phantom. It is, too, a borderland, and its explorers need to know something of the regions on both sides of the frontier. I make no claim to that double knowledge. I have merely tried, using such evidence as I can, to sketch the character of one region, that of the Romano-British civilization.

www.ingramcontent.com/pod-product-compliance
Lightning Source LLC
Chambersburg PA
CBHW022041090426
42741CB00007B/1160